ble®

ogs

Bichons Frises

by Connie Colwell Miller

Consulting Editor: Gail Saunders-Smith, PhD

Consultant: Jennifer Zablotny, DVM
Member, American Veterinary Medical Association

Capstone
press®
Mankato, Minnesota

Pebble Books are published by Capstone Press,
151 Good Counsel Drive, P.O. Box 669, Mankato, Minnesota 56002.
www.capstonepress.com

1 2 3 4 5 6 12 11 10 09 08 07

Library of Congress Cataloging-in-Publication Data
Miller, Connie Colwell, 1976–
  Bichons frises / by Connie Colwell Miller.
  p. cm.—(Pebble Books. Dogs)
  Summary: "Simple text and photographs present the bichon frise breed and
how to care for them"—Provided by publisher.
  Includes bibliographical references and index.
  ISBN-13: 978-0-7368-6697-2 (hardcover)
  ISBN-10: 0-7368-6697-3 (hardcover)
  1. Bichon frise—Juvenile literature. I. Title. II. Series.
SF429.B52M55 2007
636.72—dc22
                                                        2006020381

Note to Parents and Teachers

The Dogs set supports national science standards related to life
science. This book describes and illustrates bichons frises. The
images support early readers in understanding the text. The
repetition of words and phrases helps early readers learn new
words. This book also introduces early readers to subject-specific
vocabulary words, which are defined in the Glossary section. Early
readers may need assistance to read some words and to use the
Table of Contents, Glossary, Read More, Internet Sites, and Index
sections of the book.

Table of Contents

bichon frise (bee-SHAWN free-ZAY)

Friendly and Fluffy

Bichons frises are cuddly, friendly little dogs. They like to be near people.

Groomed bichons frises look like fluffy, white cotton balls.
Owners brush their curly, white coats into puffs.

From Puppy to Adult

Newborn bichons frises are white with pink noses. Their noses turn black after a week.

Bichon frise puppies are as big as a grapefruit. Adults are only about as tall as a basketball.

The small size of adult bichons makes doing tricks easy. Owners can teach bichons to walk on their hind legs.

Bichon Frise Care

Bichons frises need food and water every day. They also need lots of attention. Bored or lonely bichons often get into trouble.

Bichons frises do not shed their coats like other dogs. Owners should brush bichons every day. These dogs need haircuts every six weeks.

Bichons frises need baths
once a week.
Their white coats
get dirty easily.

Bichons frises make good pets.
They are smart and friendly little dogs.

Glossary

attention—playing, talking, and being with someone or something

bored—not interested in something

brush—to smooth or remove tangles from hair

coat—a dog's fur

hind—back or rear

lonely—feeling sad to be alone

shed—to lose fur

trick—a clever or skillful act

Read More

Murray, Julie. *Bichons Frises.* Dogs. Edina, Minn.: Abdo, 2003.

Preszler, June. *Caring for Your Dog.* Positively Pets. Mankato, Minn.: Capstone Press, 2007.

Internet Sites

FactHound offers a safe, fun way to find Internet sites related to this book. All of the sites on FactHound have been researched by our staff.

Here's how:

1. Visit *www.facthound.com*

2. Choose your grade level.

3. Type in this book ID **0736866973** for age-appropriate sites. You may also browse subjects by clicking on letters, or by clicking on pictures and words.

4. Click on the **Fetch It** button.

FactHound will fetch the best sites for you!

Index

Word Count: 153
Grade: 1
Early-Intervention Level: 16

Editorial Credits
Martha E. H. Rustad, editor; Juliette Peters, set designer; Kyle Grenz, book designer;
Kara Birr, photo researcher; Scott Thoms, photo editor

Photo Credits
Capstone Press/Karon Dubke, 14, 16, 18; Cheryl A. Ertelt, 8; Getty Images Inc./Workbook
Stock/SuLu Images, 12; Kent Dannen, cover, 10; Mark Raycroft, 6; Norvia Behling/Connie
Summers, 4; Photo Resource Hawaii/Tami Dawson, 20; Shutterstock/Tad Denson, 1